SPEAKING
of *Writing...*

CAROLYN EWOLDT

SCHOLASTIC
Toronto • Sydney • New York • London • Auckland

With thanks to Ginette and her parents
for permission to use her work and words

Scholastic-TAB Publications Ltd,
123 Newkirk Road, Richmond Hill, Ontario, Canada L4C 3G5

Scholastic Inc.
730 Broadway, New York, NY 10003, USA

Ashton Scholastic Pty Limited,
PO Box 579, Gosford, NSW 2250, Australia

Ashton Scholastic Limited
165 Marua Road, Panmure, P.O. Box 12328, Aukland 6, New Zealand

Scholastic Publications Ltd.
Holly Walk, Leamington Spa, Warwickshire CV324LS, England

Cover by Yüksel Hassan

6 5 4 3 2 1   Printed in USA   9/8 0 1 2 3 4/9

Canadian Cataloguing in Publication Data
Ewoldt, Carolyn, 1940—
    Speaking of writing. . .

Includes bibliographical references.
ISBN 0-590-73437-7

1.English language - Rhetoric - Study and Teaching.
2.English language - Composition and exercises -
Study and teaching. I. Title.

PE1404.E86 1989   808'.042'07   C89-095171-3

Contents

Introduction

Early in my teaching career the author Mauree Applegate spoke to me through a little nugget of wisdom contained in *Easy in English*. It shaped my thinking and even now shores up my philosophy whenever it seems in danger of sagging. I even remembered the page it was on, and recently, when I needed a way to express my philosophy, I decided that reference would be just right. So I went back to the book for the exact wording, but to my surprise, the quotation I thought was there wasn't. Obviously one or two words had triggered the idea in my mind, but Ms. Applegate never wrote the sentence I've attributed to her all these years.

Reading and writing are incredibly powerful tools of thought. But even considering the amount of work already undertaken, research into the writing process has barely begun. Donald Graves and others have helped us feel secure enough to incorporate writing instruction into the school curriculum, but the answers to questions about how best to instruct are not all in.

Actually, I hope there never will be definitive answers to every question, because much of the excitement of writing has to do with the exploration of the unknown. It remains true that all writers have to rediscover the writing process for themselves. Fortunately, our individual experiences and the meaning we make of them will always ensure that no list of how-to-teach maxims will ever satisfy every teacher and every learner.

Perhaps the idea I've prized so highly would have come to me without reading those one or two words that triggered it, perhaps not. In any case, I remain grateful to Mauree Applegate, and to Donald Graves and others who have given us permission to be learners, for having given me the forum (and courage) for thinking my own thoughts. I hope something in this book will do similar things for you.

By you I mean teachers and students both, for this book is meant to be shared. Through it I hope to engage students and teachers in dialogues meant to free them for the exploration and use of writing strategies others have described. I also invite them to develop new strategies. We should all welcome new writers into our circle, listen to their voices and discover what they can contribute to us.

I hope this book will be a catalyst for all kinds of interaction: students sharing together, and with teachers, and teachers sharing with each other. Such interactions help us articulate our own theories and translate them for others, and add to our own understanding the experiences of our collaborators, young and old, present and past.

I would especially like to thank Ginette and her classmates, Anne Marie and her classmates, and all the students and teachers with whom I've interacted through many years of teaching and learning. Even though the final composition of the book was mine, the voices in it are those of Ginette and Anne Marie.

All three of us wish you well in your roles as teachers and learners. We hope that this book will provide you with a forum for thinking your own thoughts and for coming to a better understanding of your own philosophy.

For students: thoughts about writing

Ginette writes

Just Like Them

As far back as I can remember, I always protected my sister.

She wasn't very pretty, with small eyes, a large nose and she was too tall and too big for her age. But inside, she was a beautiful person and I loved her.

Already at 10 years old, the children made fun of her and teased her. I always stuck up for her and I wondered how long it would take for her to defend herself as this was my last year at Topley Elementary. Could Sarah cope with those nasty children?

But now Dear Sarah was gone. They call it "ACCIDENTAL DEATH," but I know. I had the letter she left. They say she was swimming and got caught in the underwater current. But I know, I have the letter. She told me in that letter she was going to jump and she did. I was also told never to reveal that letter to anyone. For, in that letter holds a secret. About those mean, nasty children. The evil people who teased my best friend, who killed my best friend, my sister, only 14 years old.

I was to condemn them all with my sister and Agatha by the creek. We would have the last wicked laugh.

"It has been two weeks since Sarah left me." I wrote in my diary. "She said she'd come back. Where is she?" I put my diary down on my bed. Just then, I heard a light tapping on the door. The rythym was "Sweet Girl." Sarah's favorite melody. I got up slowly and answered the door timidly. In came Sarah, kind of floating, like a ghost, a spirit.

"Don't be frightened Crystal" said Sarah in a hollow voice.

"It is me Sarah. I want you to go to the house in the dark, foggy creek. Agatha is there. She will help you with powers. Magical Powers that will put these selfish people who hurt me through a horrid time. Do not harm them physically for I would not want you nor I to stoop to their low life level. Scare them, haunt them. Make them go so out of their minds that they will have to be institutionalized. I will never come back Crystal." Sarah's voice began to fade. "I love and trust you. Goodbye." And with that she was gone. My dear, good sister.

I cried for long time after she left. But then I thought about Agatha. I grabbed my coat and ran out the door with flashlight in hand, towards the creek.

I reached the creek within a matter of minutes. I shined my

flashlight into the darkness. I saw fog, fog and more fog. I continued to walk trying not to step into the swampy water. I finally saw the small cottage. As I went to open the door, there stood Sarah and Agatha with knives in their hands. Just as Sarah was about to throw one, there went the knife and I heard someone saying, "Crystal, wake up." I awoke to see mom standing at my bedside. I saw her eyes all red and puffy. "Crystal," she said, "Your sister went swimming today and drown." I looked up to see my mothers' face, but something caught my eye. A piece of folded up paper that read "CRYSTAL." The letter!!!!!

I knew that she would be back to haunt me, because dear Sarah, I did not protect her as in my dream. I went along with kids and called her nasty names also. I, her own sister would leave her alone while we played. Everything in the dream was like a message. I knew my sister would be back ...

Ginette, the author of this story, is a 13-year-old student in grade eight. She lives with her mother, father and younger brother in a small town in Ontario. The family speaks both French and English at home and Ginette is fluent in both languages. She enjoys baseball and collects books. She loves to read.

Ginette: *I've always read a lot of books. I was always eager to read, especially when I was younger. When I couldn't read, I wanted to rush through the alphabet and everything just so I could read because I really wanted to read.*

Ginette also likes to write. Here is one of her poems, one she considers to be among her best:

Being Alone

As the sun disappears from the bright, yellow sky,
the sparkling streams are soon running dry.

I see the dark moon come into sight,
I tremble with fear and shiver from fright.

Just now I know the time is right,
to think deeply about my fear and beliefs,
and consider my thoughts, my pain and my grief.

I sit here alone and wonder,
while I'm stuck in the rain and afraid of the thunder.

I have no home,
no pets to call my own,

no father or mother,
no sister nor brother.

I'm all alone in this big, dark world,
only me, a 13-year-old girl.

I am hungry and sad,
because no one protects me,
but I am happy and glad,
that no one takes me.

Ginette talks about her poem

During a conversation with me about her poem, Ginette pointed out several important things about writing.

> **It's all right to get help from other people.**

Ginette: *Rachel helped me a lot on this poem.*

Carolyn: *Who's Rachel?*

Ginette: *She's a girl in my class. Like, I started writing a lot of it, but she helped me with this part here and this up here.*

Carolyn: *"I see the dark moon" and "I am hungry and sad" — those parts?*

Ginette: *Yes. A lot of the people in my class write poems a lot, and they show their friends, stuff like that. Me and my friend Tammy, we've exchanged poems a couple of times, to look at them.*

> **Although friends may give you advice, you don't have to take their advice if you don't agree with it.**

Ginette: *I think everyone is entitled to their own opinion. If someone thinks it's a good story, that's their opinion. I respect it. But maybe I'll think it's something else that makes a good story. So it all depends, I guess, on the person. I don't think there's any right or wrong answer.*

> **Sometimes you need to change what you write so you can better express your thoughts and feelings.**

Carolyn: *You changed the format — the spacing — when you typed it. Any particular reason?*

Ginette: *I was thinking, you know, a bright yellow sky. Like the sun's disappearing, and it's just nightfall, and the darkness is just coming in now, so then I thought if I leave spaces, it's kind of like taking steps at a time into the night sort of thing ... Okay, here I changed it too. Right there I wrote, "I sit here alone and wonder." The first time I wrote, "I sit here all night and wonder." Okay, I thought, well, "all night" — you know it's night. And I thought, well, I wanted to emphasize that I was alone, all alone.*

Ginette considered both word choice and spacing to try to convey her ideas more precisely in her second attempt.

It helps if you can picture what you're writing in your head.

Carolyn: *What do you think the last line means?*

Ginette: *Okay, like it's not in my position at all because he's my brother over there and so I have a brother. I was just thinking — I just kind of pictured myself sitting under a tree, and it's raining, and I'm thinking about things, and I thought, well, like I'm hungry and I'm sad because no one protects me, but I'm happy and glad that no one can take me away. Like I can be myself, where I want. I can do what I want, not what everybody else wants.*

Ginette used visual imagery, like having a TV screen in her mind. She visualized herself sitting under a tree. That mental picture helped her to think about the content of the poem, as well as the words she would use to describe the scene.

You don't have to write only about your real experiences.

Ginette: *... teenagers in school and stuff like that, like real life experiences. I like to write about my own class and things we do.*

Although Ginette says that she writes best about things she knows, both her story and her poem are based on imaginary situations.

She isn't really alone in the world, like the person in the poem — her brother came into the library as we talked. Writers have choices about staying within their own real world or moving outside, or even combining elements of real experiences with imaginary ones.

Invitation

You might want to talk about Ginette's poem with your classmates. Your discussion might focus on the following:

- What did you like about the poem?
- What did the poem make you think about?
- What experiences have you had writing poetry?

Perhaps some of you could share a poem of your own with the group and discuss it in the same way.

Ginette talks about her story

A poem or story doesn't usually spill out of an author fully formed and perfect. Writing requires time and patience and a willingness to take detours.

Ginette wrote "Just Like Them" in class. In the last week of January she started to work on a story called "The Other People," but after writing only four pages she decided to start something new. She sat for a whole writing period just thinking about what to write. That story turned out to be "Just Like Them."

> **You shouldn't feel discouraged. All writers have "dry spells."**

Ginette: *And then, right at the end of the period I kind of just started on this one. When I started with this one, I guess from this one to the finished copy, I guess it took about a week and a half that I worked on it.*

Carolyn: *Does it happen often that you take a whole period to think of a topic to write about?*

Ginette: *Yes.*

Carolyn: *How do you feel about that?*

Ginette: *Well, I get frustrated sometimes because it takes so long. I'll sit in class and just kind of sit and sit and sit and think and think. Then I'll start writing a paragraph, and then I'll throw it out 'cause I don't really like that story, like it's not interesting to me. A lot of times it takes one period just to figure out a topic, and then the next day I have that topic in mind. Then I don't want to write about that anymore. So it'll keep going on for a long time.*

Ginette's teacher advises her students to keep a list of possible story topics and consult it when writing time comes. Ginette explained that her ideas come from several different sources.

> **You can use the same idea in different stories.**

Ginette started "Just Like Them" by writing the same beginning as she had used in "The Other People." Although she'd given up on the rest of the story, she liked the first line and wanted to save it:

As far back as I can remember, I always protected my sister.

A good strategy for saving ideas, names, phrases, even whole sections you like is to write them in a small notebook and copy them into another story later on. That way the time spent on an abandoned story doesn't seem wasted.

> **You can get ideas from other people.**

After that first line Ginette describes the sister in the story:

She wasn't very pretty, with small eyes, a large nose and she was too tall and too big for her age. But inside, she was a beautiful person and I loved her.

Ginette: *Okay, at this point my friend Elizabeth, she was writing a story about a little boy. And she described him, but not like this. But she was describing him sort of like the same way, so I thought I could use that.*

> **You can get ideas from books.**

Working with classmates and sharing is important, but you can also get writing ideas from books you read. Books often contain interesting ideas and styles of writing you may want to use in your own work. That doesn't mean that you copy from other authors, just that

8

they inspire you to try the kinds of things they've tried.

Ginette: *This story was my idea, but the books have helped me — different parts from different books. I'll think about it and that's how I get my ideas ... I don't copy it word for word, but I get ideas from the books a lot.*

Ginette's reading provided the source for the character of Sarah.

Ginette: *In the book I had read the child wasn't very pretty, and the children didn't tease her at school and her parents didn't tease her either, but they would whisper about her, and they didn't want to show her to anyone because she was so ugly.*

She got the idea for the character of Agatha from another book.

Ginette: *Well, I read a book about something like this ... It was about a little girl, and her mother leaves, and she goes to the creek, and this lady teaches her to do things just with her eyes, to cause accidents.*

The name Agatha came from still another book, as did the idea of seeing Sarah as a ghost.

Ginette: *The little girl was blind. She has a friend that sees this ghost of a girl named Amanda, but she never tells anyone. She just kind of ignores it, that she sees it.*

I asked Ginette about her use of the phrase "Dear Sarah" because I liked the way the character in the story used that phrase when thinking about her sister.

Ginette: *There was one book, a Sweet Valley High book, actually. There are two twins, and the sister got hit by a car, and she was in the hospital. But I don't think I got it from there. Maybe I thought about it, but I don't remember.*

Writers usually take bits and pieces from a variety of sources and use them to make a different story. Not remembering where ideas came from is typical of all writers.

> **Personal experiences can also give you ideas.**

Ginette: *And if I see something happen, I'll think about it or something related to it and I'll write about that.*

The name "Topley Elementary" came from a real school in British Columbia where Ginette's class had penpals. A camping experience inspired the flashlight.

Ginette: *During the summer I went camping, and at night whenever we'd go in the boat, we'd have a big flashlight.*

Remember how Ginette used visual imagery to help write her poem? Sometimes it's a personal experience that calls up a mental image.

Ginette: *I see a picture of some house I've been in ... how the set-up is. A lot of times like with the kitchen, my aunt's kitchen will come into my head, and that's how it is through the whole story. When someone walks in, it's always in that kitchen.*

In this case Ginette visualized the scene of a story she had read that took place in a bedroom. She drew on her mental image of that bedroom to describe the bedroom scene in her own story, picturing her characters talking and moving about in that room. She also drew on her own mental image to describe her ghost.

Ginette: *I always think of ghosts — female ghosts — kind of as wearing long, white robes, and that's how I got it for here.*

> **You can't always plan the whole story. Things change as you write.**

Ginette: *A lot of times I change the words around. Sometimes I change the sentences around, and I add things and I take out things while I write. And then this one, when I started on this, I went pretty fast, but you know, I changed a few things around too. Like I put paragraphs in different order. I took some stuff out ... With this one, everyone was asking me if I was going to start it over, put different things in it and add on to it. Some people said that I shouldn't, and some people said that I should, so what I'm going to do, maybe later on, I'm going to keep this story, but I'm going to try to add on to it, make it longer.*

Carolyn: *What do you think you'll add?*

Ginette: *Maybe I'll put in parts of when the children were teasing her* or maybe when I was sticking up for her in the dream ... Then at the end maybe I'll put in what happens to me after she comes back — because she comes back again. But it wouldn't be much longer.

Carolyn: *When you were writing this did you know all along that the main character had been unkind to her sister?*

Ginette: *No, I kind of got that at the end and thought, Wow! this would be weird if I changed it to get me to be unfaithful to my sister. I don't know. I kind of came up with it. When I was writing it, I was going to write it, like I wasn't going to make it a dream or anything. Then after I was writing it I thought about it. Why not make it a dream and then have me ... you know. In my class when you read stories, it's better to have a really weird ending. Then everyone really gets into it. So I decided to have this ending. At the beginning I wanted it to be like I was really good to her and everything, and then at the end being really nasty. When I started writing it I thought for a long time, but near the end when I got the idea about the dream and leaving her alone, I just kind of wrote like I was really inspired. I really wrote fast.*

Ginette has learned one of the thrills of writing: as we write, we sometimes discover knowledge or thoughts we never knew we had.

Invitation

Now your discussion group might focus on Ginette's story and her writing of it.

- What did you like about the story?
- What did the story make you think about?
- Should Ginette change her story in the ways she mentions above?
- Do you have any other suggestions for changes in the story, or do you think it should be left as it is?

Perhaps you can share a story of your own with the group. The others may be able to provide you with answers to questions you have about how to make your story better.

Ginette talks about her class

Ginette has always enjoyed writing at home, but this year has been a good year for writing in school because her teacher has started a process writing program in her class.

Ginette: *When I was younger I used to write stories too, but not like this. And then we started a writing program, and I was really happy about that because I like writing, and I wrote a poem first and then I wrote these.*

Each day class time is set aside for the students to write, read and publish their work. They can ask one or more classmates to help them *revise* sections they want help with. Then, using a typewriter or word processor (or their best handwriting), they *edit* their work for spelling, punctuation and capitalization and *proofread* it for publication. If they wish, they add illustrations and bind the pages into a construction paper or cardboard cover with decorations added.

They use sharing time to share their writing, and learn what makes their stories interesting to an audience. Sometimes this is called "Author's Chair" because the students sit in a chair at the front of the class.

Ginette often works on several pieces at once. She may have one story ready to publish, another half finished, a third only a topic in her mind. She may decide not to finish one. Another may turn out to be as exciting as "Just Like Them." There's only one thing that's certain: Ginette will keep writing.

But some students are afraid to write, or think they can't. I asked Ginette what advice she would give them.

Ginette: *I've never really thought about if I could do it or not. I don't think you should think about if you can do it. I think you should just do it and see how it turns out. If it doesn't turn out, well, you can always try again. Don't be afraid to try.*

Carolyn: *What do you think makes a writer a good writer?*

Ginette: *I think you have to spend time on your stories. You can't just rush through it really fast. I think you really have to think about the story. Even the words you're using, the language you're using in it.*

Ginette talks about success

Carolyn: *Do you feel "Just Like Them" is the best thing you've written this year?*

Ginette: *Yeah, this year. Well, when I first wrote it, I didn't think it was that great. I like it now, but I guess because I'm reading it so much that I'm used to it. I didn't think it was as good as everyone thought it was. I thought it was okay, but it didn't really dawn on me that it was good.*

Ginette felt shy about reading her story to her classmates and had to be encouraged to do so. When she finished, her classmates were completely silent, so impressed that they were unable to comment at first. Then they burst out to tell her how much they liked it. They were very pleased that her story was chosen to be in this book. One student observed that maybe the story wouldn't have been written if they hadn't all participated in the writing program. Ginette's success was, in a sense, their triumph too.

Even if you don't like Ginette's story as much as her classmates did, I hope this conversation about writing has helped you to understand the writing process a little more. Writing can be frustrating and difficult, but if you take the time to choose a topic that's really interesting to you, it can also be wonderful!

Ginette and I hope that we've inspired you to pick up a pen and write, write, write. Your teacher, your classmates, and all the authors who have come before you are ready to give you a hand.

For teachers: the writing process

The first chapter — Ginette's story and my discussions with her about it — are meant mainly for students, and I hope you'll distribute the book freely and help your students engage in the kinds of interactions I've suggested in the invitations.

I presented the story first, so the students could savor it for a while. Then I engaged Ginette in conversation about her poem "Being There," to show how she uses some of the same strategies in writing the poem that she uses in her story: sharing, getting ideas from her peers, making changes after the first draft, calling up visual images, and using real, imaginary and vicarious experiences as sources for her writing. Our conversations make it clear that the composing process isn't always easy and spontaneous, that a story can't always be planned out in advance. I also included invitations to the students to share their impressions of Ginette's work, to form groups to discuss their own work, and to keep writing.

In his book *Writing: Teachers and Children at Work* (1983), Donald Graves describes a process writing program in which students select their own topics to write, revise and publish for an audience beyond the teacher. This year Anne Marie, Ginette's teacher, decided to engage her class in that kind of process writing. But before we hear her share some of her strategies for fostering writing in the next chapter, I want to offer some additional perspectives on Ginette's work and to make connections between her writing and what she has to say about it.

As I mentioned, before writing "Just Like Them" Ginette began a different story, which she abandoned except for the first line: *As far back as I can remember.* When she made that the opening line of her new story, she established that as a first-person narrative as well.

> *With a lot of stories I start out saying "a person," but then as I go along I say "I" a lot, so I thought it would be easier if I just said "I" through the whole thing.*

Writers have much to attend to in any moment of composing. They must continually make decisions: about the message, about grammatical structures, about conventions of usage and of spelling and punctuation, about surface features such as letter formation and spacing, about issues of register and style. Ginette wisely gave in to her tendency to write in the first person, a stylistic feature that came easily to her, so she could direct more attention to other decisions.

Her tendency may also have been influenced, however subconsciously, by a sense of the tone, theme and threads of a plot for a story that had been evolving in her mind. Let's trace that evolution, begun perhaps already with the poem "Being Alone" which she wrote just after the Christmas holidays. Next she started work on "The Other People," but abandoned it after only four pages. That story began with a dramatic incident:

> *... and she comes home one day, and her parents are really arguing, and her father, like he's packing, and he leaves. She hides behind the bushes as he leaves and then she comes back in the house. And I was going to write it as if he had another family — but I didn't. I kind of left that one, and then I went to this one.*

A sombre, reflective tone and the theme of loneliness are found in all three pieces, and all three are written in the first person. The additional theme of betrayal, which Ginette began developing in "The Other People," is also sustained in "Just Like Them." However, in the latter the tone changes to one of mystery, and the use of the first person narrator serves a different purpose.

In both "The Other People" and "Being Alone" the first person focus allows the reader access to the main character's feelings. But in "Just Like Them" the first person is used to create distance between the main character and the reader, to deny the reader access to certain information and thereby allow for a surprise ending and a more powerful story.

I asked Ginette why she decided to stop writing the first story.

> *I don't know. I found that it would be kind of complicated to write. I didn't really like the story line because after she finds out about the other family, I didn't really know what else could happen that was interesting.*

Leaving a story unfinished shouldn't be viewed as a problem. In writing as much as she did, Ginette already achieved several things. First, she had a chance to explore a topic that was novel and difficult for her, one that required experimentation with the expression of strong emotions, which aren't easy to convey. Second, she learned that she needed to know more about handling a plot of such complexity and that she needed more depth of experience to know where such a situation might lead. Awareness of these needs will push Ginette to read more widely and be more sensitive to the demonstrations provided by other authors.

> *I think as I get older, I know more things to write about. I have a lot to learn. I think when I'm starting to read more things, like even in high school, find other books, I think I'll be a better writer.*

Smith (1988) calls this "reading like a writer" and describes how other members of the "literacy club" influence fledgling members by providing written demonstrations. Ginette draws upon several sources for her work, but still has some concern about using them.

> *Well, when I write sometimes I do come up with stuff like that, but I think, well, I shouldn't write this because maybe people'll think I got it from a book.*

Many students need reassurance on this point, even though famous authors readily acknowledge the contributions of other authors to their own development. We need to let students know that it's a permissible and valuable strategy to draw on other sources. Emerging writers don't copy word for word, but attempt to emulate elements of style, plot, theme, mood and characterization demonstrated by other authors, and we can sometimes trace the relationship of these elements from one text to another.

"Intertextual tying" is what de Beaugrande (1980) calls a reader's perception of relationships between texts. We can encourage it by helping students see similarities in stories and by reading well-written text to them.

Ginette began writing her first story in late January and completed the second one in mid February. All in all, about a month elapsed between her poem and her final story. The point has been made, but is well worth repeating: partially writing the first story facilitated Ginette's choice of tone, theme and style that came together so powerfully in "Just Like Them."

But even so, she spent a good deal of time coming up with the second story — a whole writing period, in fact. If her teacher hadn't been sensitive to the needs of authors, she might have chastised Ginette for "wasting time," or for "not finishing" what she started. A premature emphasis on product could have been detrimental to both the process and the final product.

Ginette abandoned another story later in the year because she didn't know how to end it. When she and I talked about it, I asked what would cause her to give up that story.

Oh, I don't know. Right now it's ... Maybe I'll find something better to write. Maybe I will continue it. I'm not really sure right now. I'd have to sit down and look at it, read it over a couple of times to see what I can add or what I can't add — see what I can do.

Most striking is the strong sense of ownership Ginette feels. *She* will make the decision. Not even the likelihood that other people will enjoy her story is sufficient reason, in itself, for continuing to write.

To me, I can't really write a story that I find — like, if I find it boring, I can't write it. People may like it but for me, I wouldn't want to write a story that I didn't think was interesting. And then I wouldn't let other people read it.

Yet Ginette is very aware of a reading audience. She likes sharing her work with classmates and friends. While maintaining her ownership, she also aspires to please her parents, her classmates and her brother. Their (imagined) reactions to her work help to guide her planning and revising.

Sometimes I write stories that are, I don't know, the kind of stories that the boys don't like. I kind of think, "Well, will they like this? No, they'd probably think it was dumb." So sometimes I'll change it. I'm very conscious of who reads it...

For me, being mentally hurt is worse than being physically hurt. And I thought that — I didn't want a violent person, but I wanted someone that could get their own way in the story. I didn't want a story like that with violence in it. I just wanted something that would be really strange, something that would be different...

And fourteen years old — I didn't want to make her too young. I wanted to make her old enough to understand about suicide, but not too old...

I was reading it over again and [it said], "I knew she'd be back to haunt me." I was thinking about that, and then I thought, well, could I give them something that they knew I was thinking about ... It's hard to explain.

Ginette's last comment exemplifies the role of reading in the writing process. Writers constantly reread their work to test its effect on an audience or to be reminded of what they have already said. Rereading rekindles excitement and provides the impetus to continue.

Ginette showed me an earlier draft of "Just Like Them," and because I wanted to discover the kinds of revisions she makes voluntarily and without assistance, I compared it with her final copy. Here are portions of her rough copy (originally handwritten) with her revisions in parentheses.

As far back as I can remember, I always stuck up for (protected) my sister. She wasn't very pretty. With small eyes, a large nose and she was too tall and too large (big) for (her) age. But inside she was a beautiful person, and I loved her.

Okay, "stuck up" — I thought it would be better language use, I guess, if I used "protected" instead of "stuck up for." It sounded better, I thought.

Ginette is finding her own writing voice. While she might have used "stuck up for" in conversation, she is revising on the basis of how her *writing* should sound. Graves (1983) says that each writer "... has to come to terms with the transition from speech to print." (p. 163)

A look at both rough and finished copies will determine whether an "error" shows a student's lack of understanding of a particular convention or is simply the result of transposing. The comma between *person* and *and* (above) was missing in Ginette's final draft. It's obvious that she is aware of how to use commas in compound sentences and doesn't need to be helped on that point.

Here are more excerpts from her rough copy:

But now, dear (Dear) Sarah was gone. They call it "Accidental Death," (ACCIDENTAL DEATH) but I know.
In came Sarah, kind of floating. Like a vision. (, like a ghost, a spirit.)
I was kind of scared. (This sentence was omitted in the final draft.)
"Don't be frightened Crystal." (, said Sarah in a hollow voice.)

Ginette capitalizes ACCIDENTAL DEATH because "it would stand out more if I put it larger." She knows what she wants to emphasize but is not yet able to provide the emphasis linguistically, so she emphasizes the idea graphically. She'll come across other devices for emphasis as she continues to consult other authors.

The omission of the sentence "I was kind of scared" and the addition of the dialogue carrier "said Sarah in a hollow voice" make the remaining lines stronger.

Ginette's revisions are substantive: she changes words, inserts missing words, rewords awkward phrases, provides emphasis, adds descriptive words and makes the language more economical. After all the changes to her first draft, she says, it's so messy that even she can't read it. So she always recopies it. While rewriting, she subconsciously continues to revise her work.

> *Like when I write good copies from my rough copies, I look at the rough copy, and a lot of times I'll just kind of change it as I'm writing, and sometimes I don't even realize that I'm changing it. Just — I think, you know, it might sound better like this.*

There are still errors in Ginette's final draft, as seen at the beginning of this book. Many teachers believe that a piece shouldn't be published unless it's error free. Others feel that if students have conscientiously revised as extensively as they can, their ownership should not be violated.

Is Ginette atypical — an exceptionally talented writer, amazingly articulate about the process? She had accumulated a large portfolio before her teacher started the writing program. Clearly she'd been thinking about her own writing process longer than most of her fellow students. But I would like to suggest that most students will write and share their writing, as Ginette did, if you provide a risk-free environment where you and they work together to gain better control over and understanding of the writing process.

A process writing program

After teaching grade eight for one year in a small Catholic school in a Toronto suburb, Anne Marie decided that she needed help with her writing program and began taking a course toward her Reading Specialist degree. That's how we met.

I assigned Donald Graves' *Writing: Teachers and Children at Work* as a key text. Anne Marie first thought that process writing and whole language would work only in the lower grades, but as she continued reading Graves, she began to see that the writing process applied to older writers in many ways as well.

Deciding to initiate process writing in her class wasn't easy for her, a relatively new teacher and the only one in the upper grades interested in trying it. Furthermore, she had only 40 minutes a day for language arts, a very short time for writing, reading, read-aloud and satisfying the school's requirement for media studies and religion.

In a whole language classroom, the whole day can easily be taken up using reading and writing as tools for curriculum subjects: science, environmental studies, music, art and so on. But with the school on a rotary system, Anne Marie couldn't integrate the curriculum that way. She had to figure out how she could cram everything that should be included into a block of 40 minutes. In this chapter we'll follow her efforts to develop the kind of program she'd come to believe was best for her students.

In the same way they are evolving as writers, I am evolving as their teacher.

Anne Marie's class contained a typically wide range of writing abilities. She told me that some students were already composing stories that were better than anything she herself could produce, while others still needed work on writing complete sentences.

What was her writing program like before she read Graves' book?

Before my conversion? [She laughed.] In terms of language we did a lot of novel studies and question-and-answer kinds of things. Creative writing, as such, was sort of once a week. A lot of their creative writing things came from the novels, but it was always teacher directed and teacher imposed.

She simply provided her students with the kind of education she herself had received. Twice, however, Anne Marie had attempted more open assignments that gave the students some choices about what they would write, and she had seen some success. Her first attempt encouraged her students to produce pop-up books.

It was a long process, and there were many times that I wanted to give it up. I thought, "This can't be working. This can't be working." But then I saw a glimpse of it at the end when the kids saw the books. We had done them on the computer and they worked, and they were printed, and their name was on it ... and so I sort of thought, well, maybe it's sort of worthwhile.

Ownership and sharing

Although she didn't use the word then, Anne Marie was observing her students' first experience with ownership, their power to make decisions about their own writing. Their pride in their accomplishments made her feel good and provided enough encouragement for her second attempt.

She had read to students a book called *I Am David* (Holm, 1963) about a boy's journey through Europe in search of his mother.

In the last few words of the book he says, "I am David," and she says, "My son," and then it ends. The kids were very much up in arms about this: "Well, how does she explain the years that they've been apart?" And I said, "Then write how you think it should have ended." And because they were so interested in the novel, their stories were wonderful.

This had happened just before Christmas, and Anne Marie started her new writing program after the Christmas holidays. At first the students good-naturedly referred to themselves as guinea pigs, because Anne Marie confided in them that she was taking a course and that she wasn't sure of what she was doing. Often she made changes, as her understanding of the process writing approach grew and she reflected on how her students were reacting.

I told them in January we were going to start this new writing program and we were going to use their folders. They've always liked their folders, but we just never used them. You know, they were sort of over on the shelf and sometimes they'd go over and look at them. But there wasn't really much in them, even from grade seven when they first get their folders. So I told them that we'd have one section for their ideas and their topics and the middle section was where they would put the things they were working on, and the last section would be their published work.

She explained that they would have a writing time every day and that they could write about anything they liked. That announcement was startling to students who had always been told what to write. Their response was equally surprising to Anne Marie.

They made a list of their topics to put in the left-hand side of their folder, and I was amazed at the kids. I was really wondering, "Is this going to work with them?" The things they put down on their list! Like, no problems whatsoever. They had plenty of things they were going to be excited about, and they couldn't wait to start. And the next day, all day, it was, "When's the writing time?" I was totally amazed. I never, ever heard this from kids before, especially in intermediate.

Anne Marie asked her students for two finished pieces by a certain date.

Some of them were a little bit slow to start. The other ones that write anyway were just off and running, and then the few that I wasn't too sure how it would go with started too and just wrote for forty minutes, and there wasn't a sound in the classroom, and I had to stop them because we had French. And it was, "Do we have to stop?" And I thought, "This must be working."

The students signed up for a chance to share their work with classmates on Friday afternoons. Usually everyone shared with one other individual and four people shared with the whole group. Anne Marie made a rule that the students had to keep track of the classmates they shared with and rotate them so that eventually each story would be read by each student.

At first, for fear of chaos, Anne Marie focused her attention on logistics and rules, opting for a great deal of structure. Later, structural concerns fell away as she and her students became more comfortable with the program, but some rules and a consistent environment are still important to her.

What I needed to get myself organized was more of a routine or something. There were so many days that I didn't know where we were going or what people were doing. [She laughed.] It seemed that sometimes some of them were goofing off and I thought, "Is this right? Should it be more structured? Are they goofing off because I don't have it more structured?" But there were so many things that I was still trying to iron out for myself. Not structured so it's stifling, but just structured for the running of it.

Ginette agreed that some rules are important.

Everyone knows they have to be quiet when they write. She [the teacher] doesn't come out and say it, but it's kind of the thing that we know — that we have to be quiet. And that helps me, too, because it's easier to think about what I want to write when it's quiet instead of talking and everything around me. Because I can't concentrate when people around me are talking, so that helps.

Calkins (1983) talks of the facilitative effects of "the juxtaposition of a complex, changing craft such as writing and a simple consistent environment." (p. 32) By not keeping the environment consistent, Anne Marie found that the Friday afternoon sharing time "sort of fell by the wayside. And that's one thing that I wish hadn't because that was a real important time for them in terms of ownership."

Ginette echoed these feelings about the value of formal sharing time.

Like we only do it once a month now where we share our stories. I think I'd like to hear more of the stories, to see what other people are writing too. Compare our stories sometimes.

Even so, the program evoked a great deal of informal sharing.

I saw a lot of sharing — they were so excited to share their stories with each other. "Read this part of my story. What do you think about this?" And that's even increased since then. Like they can't wait in the morning. "Will you read my story?" "Will you read this part of my story?" "Will you tell me what you think?" And with each other too. They're always buzzing around, asking each other.

When formal sharing time occured, the students spontaneously began reading their stories from the stool used by Anne Marie when she read to them. Anne Marie described the audience as "mesmerized." At first students were reluctant to offer suggestions to their classmates, simply commenting that each story was good. It took a while before some began to ask questions about what they hadn't understood about a story, and then their comments reflected the kinds of things Anne Marie had said to them in one-on-one writing conferences.

She found that the wonderful ideas students often had sometimes didn't come out on paper, and she commented that many of their stories would never have happened without talking. When students talk about their stories they come to understand the need to provide sufficient information for their audience. This kind of sharing has benefits for both the developing and the talented writer. Presenting what one knows is one of the best ways to learn even more.

Responding

But responding to stories can be tricky. Fledgling writers can be hurt by a teacher's comments and by teacher-like comments from other students. Perl and Wilson (1986) describe instead a "say back" or "active listening" technique. In essence, the students say to each other, "What I hear you saying in your piece is ..." This allows them to point out areas of ambiguity and match interpretations with the author without criticizing the work.

It wasn't too difficult for Anne Marie to respond to the writing of less able students. She had lots of advice to give them: try writing a different kind of story; try using certain stylistic devices they had been experimenting with, such as figurative language; try creating vivid images through the use of strong verbs and precise language; try enlivening characters through the use of dialogue.

Many times, however, her students didn't need specific guidance, just reassurance that they'd achieved what they set out to achieve. As Hunt (1987) says, often the best responses simply make students aware that their writing has evoked an emotion in their readers.

On the whole, Anne Marie felt she had little to offer students like Ginette. I asked Ginette to describe a writing conference and tell me the kinds of things Anne Marie might say to her.

She just asks us to come and show her our story, and she asks us what we think we're gonna do next, and she kind of gives us ideas on what she's heard or what she thinks we should do. Like she doesn't tell you to do it, but she just kind of gives you ideas and they kind of build up.

24

As an example, Ginette described a conference dealing with a story about the Bermuda Triangle, when Anne Marie told her about the theories that had been suggested for the disappearance of aircraft.

All I did basically for her was praise her stories. She always handed in typed stories that were lovely to read. They were wonderful stories. A few times, you know, I'd say to her I could tell something had been whipped off and then handed in, and I'd say, "You know, this isn't your best," and she'd say "No." And she'd admit it, and she had run out of time or whatever. But there was nothing that I could say to her to do better. Like she was just a very good writer. She had all the mechanical things. She had all the ideas ... There was really nothing.

I once raised the following question with Anne Marie and some other teachers: What, if anything, can a teacher do for students who already seem to have a good understanding of the writing process?

One suggestion was to put them in contact with a willing mentor — a professional writer, perhaps a journalist or a children's book author. Another was to hold a Young Authors Conference. These are becoming popular today and can be very stimulating for young writers, although some students don't feel comfortable discussing their work with strangers they meet on only that one occasion.

A final suggestion was that talented writers should be published. Anne Marie reminded us all of her time limitations, yet she feels that publication is important for any student.

For some of them it was just an achievement for them to be writing and to feel good about their writing, or to be excited about their writing. And this even went further once we started to actually make the books. And once they went on computer — the first books they did — it took forever, but they all did their stories on the computer. And then we made the books and bound the books, and I had a book box, and they all went in there.

The books were decorated by the students, with a dedication page at the front and an "About the Author" page at the back, a short biographical sketch written by a classmate who interviewed the author about hobbies and family.

The teacher's role

I wondered if Ginette had other ideas about how her teacher could facilitate her progress in writing.

> *I think she could read us stories that she likes ... or maybe what she expects of us. There's different things she expects from different people in our class, and I think she should maybe give us some examples of stories that she really likes, what appeals to her.*

Although Anne Marie reads to her class often, being exposed to quality literature wasn't sufficient at this point for Ginette.

Carolyn: *Do you think your teacher has a better sense of what makes a good story than you do?*

Ginette: *I guess so. I've always thought that a teacher knows more than me ... I guess she does. Well, she's been writing longer, probably. I don't know if she writes stories. I don't think so. Maybe she does, but she's never shared them with us. I think she probably knows more about writing than I do.*

If teachers write and regularly share their work with students, they are viewed as partners rather than critics, as learners themselves rather than dispensers of knowledge. Anne Marie knew she should be writing stories and sharing them, but she had never felt really comfortable with writing, even though she had a degree in English.

> *It [writing in university] was always essays, and any time we had to do anything creative, I felt very hesitant and very anxious, and so I think I communicated that a lot to the kids.*

That's an important point: she had probably communicated her own insecurities to her students. It's interesting, however, that Anne Marie and Ginette each expressed a belief that the other had a greater knowledge of writing.

Ginette: *I think she knows how creative each one of us is in the class and then she marks on creativity.*

Anne Marie: *It's funny how they think that I just know everything.*

Even though she'd been keeping a journal since she was in high school, Anne Marie had never thought of that as "real writing." She confessed that she still wasn't comfortable with herself as a writer when she finally did share a piece of her own writing. When her students asked to hear what she had written during a writing period, she protested at first that she hadn't been writing a story, just "jotting down what was happening in the room." But they still wanted to hear it. This is a portion of what she had written:

> As I look around I see the paper cranes we've made. I've got to get the rest of them hung up. I like the way they move when the air hits them — the colors are so bright. I often look at the gold one Chris made and think of *Sadako and the 1000 Cranes* ... Some kids are like the cranes — easily folded — bright colored — meaning in personality. Some are still a bit crumpled — learning to find their way.

> *I felt like I would cry when I read it to them. And I thought, "This must be how they feel." I couldn't believe how nervous I felt. The only thing I had written to them before, that I shared, were their report cards, and that wasn't really to them.*

Anne Marie probably contributed a great deal more to Ginette's growth as a writer than she gave herself credit for. For instance, you may recall Ginette's use of visual imagery. Anne Marie had talked at length with her students about visual imagery.

> *I'd say, "You want to create a picture ... You know what's going on in your head, but the person reading your story is not too sure. You're the one that's the expert. But you have to communicate everything you see." A lot of times I would just say, "You're creating a picture. If you're describing a scene, what does it look like?"*

She also used the idea of visual imagery in her instructions about paragraphing.

> *I said, "Use the image of you as a movie director, and any time the action is switching or any time the scene is changing, or any time somebody else is coming on the stage, that should be a clue to you that you're going to have to switch your paragraphs."*

Even though Ginette seems to have used visual imagery before hearing about it in class, her teacher's endorsement undoubtedly helped her feel that she was free to use this strategy. (Some students think it's cheating to use strategies that haven't been the focus of instruction.)

Visual imagery helps students to clarify their experiences for themselves and for others. But some writers have told me that they recall scenes and emotions better through sound — for instance, through a piece of music. We also need to explore strategies that allow other senses to evoke memories, provoke messages and invoke reactions.

Strategies can be presented quickly at the beginning of a writing period, in "mini-lessons" that relate to such things as topic choice, conference participation, classroom procedures or rehearsal and revision. Calkins (1986) recommends that teachers provide mini-lessons on the qualities of good writing:

> ... teachers of writing need to be students of writing. We need to read the best literature we can find, we need to study what works in our own texts and in those of others. We also need to invite our students to do the same. (p. 193)

Anne Marie says that she now spends about seven minutes per day on a mini-lesson: some rule of punctuation, sentence formation or paragraphing, etc., and she considers each a good review for some students and essential information for others.

But students won't consistently apply standard writing conventions. In the heat of composing, the message will take most of the writer's attention. All of us, no matter how well versed in the rules of grammar, are likely to produce imperfect first drafts. Even beyond first drafts, however, writers often leave errors in. They already know the message well and have a hard time seeing their own misspellings and mispunctuations. Anne Marie has made the sensible rule that each student should ask four or five peers to proofread a composition before handing it in.

Evaluation

Evaluation was a major problem for Anne Marie. She looked to me for answers, but as she candidly (and rightly) commented later, "Carolyn was no help." I had my own concerns at the time about grading the students in my university classes. So she set about finding her own solution.

At first, she decided not to mark her students' stories at all. She told them she would simply look at each one and write down her feelings and comments about it in a journal. Then she would meet with the student individually, and together they would set up goals for the next piece.

*And then the next set of stories came in, and I had a binder with
every kid's name and the date and their story. And what I'd started
to do is, I was writing what I would write on the kid's paper and
then what I would write on my paper. Sometimes I wasn't too sure.
Like I'd be making more specific comments on the kid's paper, but
it was more the critical aspects of it, not so much the good things I
liked about the story. So then what I started to do was I took off the
last page of the kid's story and [put] carbon paper [behind it] so
that what I was writing to the kid was also in my journal. So that I
could say, "OK. This is what I said. This is what I liked and what
needed to be worked on."*

In time, those comments came to be more valued than actual
marks, and Anne Marie found herself filling the "comments" box on the
report cards. Much of what she wrote came from her journal entries.

She decided to give two grades to each paper. A "mechanics" grade
was influenced by the goal-setting sessions and her understanding of
what a particular student should be able to accomplish by the end of
grade eight: paragraphing, sentence structure and quotation marks
were items she specifically mentioned. A "creativity" grade was more
difficult to arrive at, as Anne Marie readily acknowledged.

*Like who am I to, you know, sit and judge. OK, so he can use
sentences. I can mark that, but I can't mark creativity or their ideas
or — this is something that's come from themselves. That's like
somebody marking, you know, how I dress or — something
personal about me, and that's not fair to do. But it's because I have
to put a grade on their report card.*

She averaged the two grades to yield one mark for each paper, but
she still felt uncomfortable about assigning a grade, so she hit upon an
idea for arriving at a modified grade for some students.

*Content-wise, what should be there at a grade eight level, in terms
of the class and then in terms of the kids themselves? There are
some kids that could never ever write at grade eight level. If I put
an E on their paper every time because they're below grade level,
they're never going to write for me ... I can put on their report card
that their language program has been modified. So I'm sort of
modifying it in terms of my expectations of the class but also my
expectations of the child.*

Her one worry was how the following year's teachers would interpret her marks. She hoped that her written comments would be given more weight than the actual grades.

She found support in Nancie Atwell's *In the Middle* (1987), which helps translate the work of Donald Graves and others to the needs and concerns of this age group. It confirmed her growing sense that evaluation ought not to be tied to specific pieces of writing but to the writing process as a whole, and be based on improvement over a term or a year's work. From this perspective, writing folders become more than receptacles for storage; they also provide longitudinal documentation of a writer's efforts.

Self-evaluation

Anne Marie had commented earlier that, even when students had little to put in them, they always liked their writing folders. But when they began to decorate them and stuff them with ideas, checklists, works in progress and finished pieces until they became dog-eared and limp from frequent handling, the students developed an overwhelming sense of ownership that reached beyond the folders themselves to encompass the whole writing process. Self-evaluation became a critical part of the writing program. As Atwell points out, helping students become aware of their own growth as writers is an important step toward the ultimate goal of any teacher: the development of confident and self-critical writers.

Ginette knew when she hadn't done her best, but she seemed less able to determine when her work was good. She didn't think "Just Like Them" was very good until others told her it was. On our own, we tend to see our faults more readily than our strengths, which is why Anne Marie feels that the sharing component of her writing program is so valuable. Her students were writing for each other and learned to commend each other's strengths, and for Anne Marie this was more important than the grades she was putting on their papers.

The growth of self-evaluation is also important because a teacher needs the student's input to evaluate any piece fairly. In the first place, it's easy for any reader to misunderstand any author's intent. In the second place, it's impossible for adults to completely understand children. However good the children are as writers, their work will be essentially childlike. Adults were children once, it's true, and teachers especially may have made a serious study of child psychology and development and spent years working among children, but they're still adults. Their childhood memories are shaped by adult perceptions, by adult knowledge, and by an adult conception of what is childlike. For most adults it's absolutely impossible to see as a child sees, unclouded by maturity and not through a mirror of assimilated experience (a paraphrase of Douglas, 1975, p. 268).

Conferences and record-keeping

Anne Marie's conferences with her students were therefore vitally important. She would plan a *process* conference for some time during the writing of a piece, and a *product* conference after the finished piece was handed in. However, it didn't always work out that neatly.

Sometimes I'd conference with them about a story, but that wouldn't be the one they would hand in to me. They would have changed their mind in between times and then handed in something else to me, which I would never have seen and never have spoken to them about. So then, things I might write down would be things that I would have talked about had we had a conference about that story.

She has now adopted the Status Report Form mentioned in Atwell's book. (p. 91) At the beginning of each writing period she asks each student for a two- or three-word response to the question: "What are you working on today?" Typical responses are: "Draft two of my poem," "Putting my story on computer," "Conferencing with my friend," "Finding a partner to proofread my story."

Anne Marie records the responses on the form, which has a column for each day of the week and a row for each student, so she can look at the whole week at one time and see how each student is progressing. She can plan an additional *process* conference with any students who have changed stories in midstream, and can keep track of low-volume writers. All that takes only about five minutes of class time at the beginning of the writing period.

She also provides an individual goal-setting sheet at each *product* conference, on which the student writes the teacher's goals for the next piece, as well as his or her own goals. The sheet is kept in the writing folder and used at the next *process* conference to determine whether goals are being met and progress is being made. When specific goals have been achieved, the student adds them to an ongoing list of writing accomplishments, which provides a checklist for proofreading.

Record-keeping is essential with so many things happening during the writing period. Students can do most of it, and keep the records in their writing folders, but you'll need to devise systems that will meet your own need for order. You might start with the forms Atwell suggests, but you'll probably modify them and creatively(!) design your own to satisfy your unique style and situation.

Problems and rewards

Anne Marie remains frustrated with the small amount of time allotted to the language arts program. She alleviates the problem somewhat by combining all the subjects she teaches the same students into one time block. This means that some days some subjects receive short shrift, but she doesn't worry about that since her writing program seems to be working so well. It seems clear that some day she will look at the possibility of integrating language arts with other subjects.

Was Anne Marie's first year of process writing worth all the anxiety: the low moments when she wondered if she was doing the right thing? the frenzied moments when she felt out of control? the lonely moments when she realized that none of the other teachers were in sync with her efforts?

I asked Ginette, who replied:

Oh, yeah. I think — yeah, a lot of [the kids] are doing a lot better this year, writing good stories ... they're kind of excited because they think they're pretty good.

Anne Marie's own answer was:

I think everyone has made progress ... I never thought kids in grade eight would be so excited about something like this. But, you know, to look at their books and to see the progress that has been made from kids that would never ever write to kids that have written a wonderful story ... There is a big guy who's taller than I am, you know, and running around saying, "Look at what I did!"

Complements to process writing

Anne Marie put a process writing program into motion despite her own uncertainties and insufficient time. As she learns and develops, she'll need to make that program more well rounded. For instance, there are many different kinds of writing, used for different purposes, and students should have opportunities to use them all.

What Anne Marie's class was producing was mostly *poetic* writing, stories and poems about someone or something external to the writer. Although Ginette's poems and stories are first person, they remain *poetic* because they are not about her own life. *Expressive* writing is personal, I-centered writing, in which the "I" maintains its own identity. *Expressive* writing is found in personal letters and journals (Britton et al., 1975).

Dialogue journals

Before process writing came to this grade eight classroom, the students wrote daily in their dialogue journals. Anne Marie responded, but the benefits didn't seem to reach those students who needed it most.

> *Before, they had to hand in one every day, and it was the same sort of drib-drab everyday that they were writing, just because I told them they had to write it. For some kids it was the same thing all the time: "Hi, how are you? I am fine." And then I would get lazy, too, and not comment back. And I found that the kids who were really enjoying the journals I enjoyed reading more, so I was able to comment more with those.*

Many students continued to keep dialogue journals after the introduction of process writing, even though Anne Marie had decided not to make them mandatory anymore. She found a decrease in quantity, but the quality improved materially. Obviously, the students chose to write when they had something to say, instead of writing whether they had anything to say or not. They were also learning to choose topics better. They were beginning to realize that they were the experts on topics closely related to their own lives, and that they had things to talk about they hadn't previously recognized. Most importantly, they were feeling that the message of their writing was being valued more than the form.

Particularly in classrooms where fiction is the predominant genre, journals provide students with a direct outlet for their personal feelings and an audience for their life experiences, whether they be dialogue journals they share or personal journals they maintain exclusively for themselves.

Journal writing can become a satisfying life-long habit. Anne Marie still values the journal she kept through high school and university, and I recently discovered the value of keeping one myself. My journal became my best friend when I went alone on a six-week trip to Australia and New Zealand that included several waits for planes and a few lonely evenings. I saved many expensive long-distance calls I might otherwise have made. And when I returned home, I possessed a lasting record of my adventures and my reactions to them.

Reading logs

Anne Marie also experimented with reading logs and was very satisfied with the results.

> *I didn't give them a list of questions. I said, "You just divide your novel up, read it and then respond. Tell me what you like about it, what you think is going to happen next. What about this character? What do you see as you read?" and so on. We called them their response journals, and so any time if we watched a movie or if we read something in class, I'd say, "Take out your response journals and just respond."*

Reading logs allow students to respond safely to literature before being asked to respond publicly. I take issue with those teachers who require that reading logs be turned in for grades. Students may use their reading logs as the basis for a formal paper, but they should be allowed to have their thoughts ferment and mellow privately through several drafts.

Poetry

Anne Marie felt that she hadn't sufficiently emphasized poetry in her class. Her students weren't writing enough of it, and they often sacrificed meaning for a rhyme scheme, perhaps believing that poetry has to rhyme.

You will give your students excellent preparation if you read them examples of good poetry often, so they see your own valuing of it. You can also stimulate their responses to poetry through reading logs.

Reading to students

Anne Marie read at least six novels to her students over the course of the year. How did she select them?

Some of them were through [book clubs]. When they send us the order forms, you get these little write-ups ... Sometimes I started reading a book and we didn't like it so we'd stop. Or books that had been read to me that I liked. It was sort of, you know, a mishmash of things. Around Christmas time I'd read them a lot of Christmas short stories, or at Halloween we looked at a lot of picture books. They like to have the picture books read to them.

She didn't always finish every book she started. Even when you preread a book you plan to read to the students, you can't always accurately predict their reception of it. Anne Marie demonstrated to her students that they, too, had a stake in class reading time — very important for older students especially, who might feel that being read to robs them of their independence. Students often feel it's taboo to leave a book unfinished, and yet all adults exercise that right in their private reading. We all encounter mandatory reading material in our lives, but when we have choice, we exercise it. Students should feel confident about doing the same.

Anne Marie read books that had been read to her. All of us are attracted to books that have been endorsed in some way by those whose opinions we respect. Once Anne Marie finished reading a novel while two students were away, and when they returned and started asking questions about how the story ended, she casually replied, "The book is over on the shelf."

And I didn't think they'd go and get it, but they did. The two of them sat there in the corner and read the last two chapters, and I thought that was neat to see.

Her students were interested in picture books. It takes a sensitive approach to read what might be perceived by adolescents as "baby books," but a few examples will prove that the books are highly enjoyable, beautifully written and illustrated, and far from "babyish." Perhaps her students' experience of making pop-up books and reading them to the grade one class had already convinced them.

Other

This list of suggestions is by no means comprehensive; the more uses and outlets for writing you can provide, the better. Nor have I included ideas for incorporating the other language arts — reading, speaking, listening, viewing — although I've made references to them all. And I've only mentioned in passing another important school topic: integration of content areas. This book simply seeks to create a forum for dialogue, and I hope that the very omission of these other important areas will stimulate more dialogue.

Looking to the future

It was only natural that Ginette and Anne Marie focused on the future in our last talks together, on writing in high school especially. Ginette was less concerned for herself than for some of her classmates. She predicted that there wouldn't be time for process writing and that they would be expected to write essays rather than stories.

I asked her if she thought her classmates would continue to write as they had this year.

No, I don't think a lot of them will. I think some of them will write a few odd stories — like even when we didn't do it [in class], I used to write stories, but I don't think a lot of them will do that ... I don't think they [the teachers] really have a lot of time to help each student individually on their stories.

Anne Marie worried that her students wouldn't yet completely understand the benefits of continuing to write, and that they hadn't had enough practice in using conventional spelling and grammar through real writing. She had heard her high school colleagues say that their students didn't know how to write proper essays, and she wondered if she should have spent time instructing her students in essay writing on assigned topics.

Yet she felt good about what she had been able to accomplish, and was proud of her students and the community they had created together.

Well, I don't have the time to do much more with them. I really wish it had started earlier. But I think in the time since January that ... every kid has at least one book now. And they feel happy, you know? They've written several stories. Their folders are something that they're proud of now. Their folders are something that they use and they're not afraid of, and they have a real sense of ownership with these folders, whereas before they were like something that belonged to me, that were on the shelf. Now it's theirs. So I think in the time I had I did as much for the kids as I possibly could.

I asked her to single out one thing teachers would need to know to implement a program such as hers.

That no matter how hard it is and how many times you want to say forget it, that it's best to stick with it. The rewards are there, but you might not see them. That's what I kept saying, "Well, I'm not seeing it; I'm not seeing it." But I see it now compared to January. That the rewards are there for you as the teacher and for the kids, too.

Theoretical and practical issues

My talks with Anne Marie and Ginette touched on a number of issues much discussed these days by both teachers and teachers of teachers. I want to offer my opinions on some crucial ones, most of them solidly grounded in the small bibliography at the end of this book. But in the end, all I can offer is some support in your search for answers. You'll need to make your own decisions.

Sharing

Atwell (1987), Graves (1983) and Calkins (1983) all feel that sharing should be part of each writing period. It helps writers to know what their classmates are doing and gives each writer a sense of audience and the feeling of ownership so critical for honesty and creativity. Sharing also gives teachers a chance to demonstrate various kinds of responses to writing.

Of course sharing is important, but share when and how? Anne Marie had a rule that, over time, every student had to share with every other individual in the class. Ginette expressed a wish that her classmates could have done more sharing with the whole class as well.

Perl and Wilson (1986) found that some students preferred to work with a small group of classmates throughout the year. These consistent groupings enabled them to develop routines and a style of interacting that facilitated their writing. One commented that she began to recognize the authors of pieces without seeing their names on the work.

But perhaps the crux of the issue lies in Anne Marie's concern that she didn't have enough class time for sharing. In practice there must be a trade-off between trying everything and providing a predictable structure within which students can concentrate on writing. Anne Marie now provides a quiet corner of the classroom for those people who want to share their work, as advocated by Harste, Short and Burke (1988). It's available at any point in the process or at any time during the writing period.

How will you organize sharing time?

Publishing

Publishing has many of the same benefits as sharing, particularly audience awareness and ownership. But publishing, too, takes time.

Graves (1983) recommends that young children publish one piece out of four or five written, older students one out of two, since their work takes longer to complete. However, you need to weigh several factors before deciding how often your students should publish and how sophisticated the publishing process should be. Pride of ownership is fostered by producing beautiful, sturdy bound books, or nicely illustrated poems for the bulletin board, but glossy appearances shouldn't take the place of quality writing. Time for publication must not rob from essential composing time.

Nor should an undue emphasis on "correctness." If students are required to edit out every error, publishing may work to destroy the power of ownership it's credited with providing. I like Anne Marie's rule that four or five students look at a piece before it's published. But even within a safe environment, some writers may be extremely sensitive to someone else's criticisms. We should always ask ourselves if our concern for product is getting in the way of the writing process.

> **How often will your students publish?**
> **How sophisticated will the publication process be?**
> **How perfect do you want the final product?**

Conferencing

Since Anne Marie could conference with her students only about once every two weeks, she took to writing copiously on the last page of each student's paper as a substitute for the product conference. She feels that this approach helps students become more aware that their writing has to make sense to a reader who can't ask for help from the author. She reserves the margins for compliments and the back page for suggestions for improvement. Some teachers, however, think that writing anywhere on student papers is a violation of the right of ownership. Some others use Post-its that students can easily remove if they find the written comments an intrusion.

But Anne Marie, realizing the danger that written comments on products might take precedence over face-to-face encounters with students, feels that both *process* and *product* conferences are necessary. It's too easy to revert, under pressure of time, to a style of teaching we want to break away from. Teaching with a stream of information flowing from "us" to "them" can sometimes seem very appealing. We have to constantly ask ourselves whether our educational decisions are consistent with the theory we profess and a true departure from practices we've learned to deem inadequate.

> **How will you find the time for conferencing?**
> **What will you say to students about their work?**
> **If you write to them about their work, what will you write and where?**

Goal-setting

At first Anne Marie set most of the goals for her students, through the suggestions she wrote on their papers. Their grades reflected her estimation of how well they had achieved her goals.

Now she makes much more room for their own goal-setting. In some senses she *does* know more about writing than her students and can help them identify improvements to reach for. On the other hand, there are problems with setting specific goals, even with those set by the students themselves. Writing should be allowed to veer off in unexpected directions.

Graves (1983) recommends that one goal be addressed in each writing conference. Even so, if you select a particular writing convention for attention, can you be sure the student is ready to understand the rule in question? Some teachers wait until they see that a student is successfully using a convention and then set a goal the "consistent use" of that convention.

> **How will goal-setting be accomplished in your classroom?**

Evaluation

Anne Marie did a great deal of soul-searching and agonizing about evaluation and readily admits to a continued concern for the fairness of her marking system.

> *Because it was so easy before — you were locked into marks. You just had to mark all the time. And you just punched the numbers into your calculator and then transferred that to a grade and stuck it on the report card. Grades are very important to these kids at this age. You know, they have to have a grade for everything. Maybe that's just because they've been trained or ... [sigh] ...*

Harste, Short and Burke (1988) say, " ... we have continued to work on new and better forms of evaluation" (p. 65). Hansen (1987) states, "Evaluation is the stickiest topic in this book."

> **What are your concerns about marking?**
> **How will writing be evaluated in your class?**

The purpose of your writing program

Anne Marie's class wrote fiction. Both Ginette and her teacher expressed concern that she and her classmates would probably be expected to write essays (expressive writing) rather than fiction in high school. I'm not clear why Anne Marie's students chose to write stories (poetic writing) almost exclusively. Perhaps it was her terminology, calling all pieces of writing "stories." Or perhaps they had simply never had an opportunity to write fiction before in their school career.

Would those students have been better prepared for high school if they had written non-fiction — essays and research papers — in grade eight? In Perl and Wilson's book (1986, p. 56), teacher Audre Allison wonders whether she should let her students simply write or whether she should prepare them for the New York Regents Examinations. All I can offer you is her questions and an invitation to help me and others think through the issues:

What are we training students to do: figure out what sells, what people in authority want, what people in authority think is true, useful, interesting? What are we teaching them: how to succeed, to adapt, to perform? Do we reward their shrewdness and ability to conform? Or do we encourage them to find their honest centers, to release their own creative energy, to love themselves?

> **How do you feel about student selection of topics?**
> **Is writing essays important for your students?**
> **Will there be a place for fiction writing in your program?**

Process writing vs. writing process

Graves (1983) and others cited in the bibliography use the term *process writing* for the kind of program described in this book, where "process" stresses fluidity, flexibility, collaboration, writing for real human purposes.

Unfortunately, any pedagogical approach can be turned into a mechanistic procedure by people who don't understand its philosophy. Graves himself warns us against becoming too orthodox in our acceptance and adherence to the approach. If process writing becomes an invariant lock-step procedure that adheres to rigid criteria for number and frequency of publications and time allowed for each conference, creativity will be stifled and writing will become a bore.

Rigid interpretations of process writing make it vulnerable to critics. For instance, Gutteridge (1988) denounces process writing for its exclusive attention to the *expressive* mode. But there's ample room for flexibility. Often teachers take an all-or-nothing approach to any new idea. I was told that one school no longer uses the language experience approach "because we do process writing here." But neither I nor anyone represented in the bibliography advocates that we rob students of any opportunity to experience the richness of language.

> **What does *process writing* mean to you?**

Loneliness

Anne Marie had no colleague in her school who also used process writing. She couldn't share her new experiences and had to face the criticisms of teachers who still believed that process writing was only for the lower grades. She had to face self-doubts and forge a new trail on her own.

> *See, I was the only one here that was doing it. And so that was hard, too, because I didn't have anybody to go to and say, "Well, what do you think?"*

The good news is this: there is support if you look for it. You'll find it in colleagues from other schools, in books, in the achievements of your students. Perhaps a first step in implementing a writing program should be to decide where your support and inspiration will come from.

> **Where will *your* support come from?**

References

Applegate, M. *Easy in English*. New York: Harper & Row, 1960.

Atwell, N. *In the middle: writing, reading, and learning with adolescents*. Portsmouth, NH: Heinemann, 1987.

Britton, J., T. Burgess, N. Martin, A. McLeod and H. Rosen. *The development of writing abilities (11-18)*. London: Macmillan, 1975.

Calkins, L. *The art of teaching writing*. Portsmouth, NH: Heinemann, 1986.

Calkins, L. *Lessons from a child*. Portsmouth, NH: Heinemann, 1983.

de Beaugrande, R. *Text, discourse, and process: toward a multi-disciplinary science of texts*. Norwood, NJ: Ablex, 1980.

Douglas, W. "On value in children's writing," in R. Larson, ed., *Children and writing in the elementary school*. Toronto: Oxford University Press, 1975.

Graves, D. *Writing: teachers and children at work*. Portsmouth, NH: Heinemann, 1983.

Gutteridge, D. *The dimension of delight: A study of children's verse writing, ages 11-13*. London, ON: The Althouse Press, 1988.

Hansen, J. *When writers read*. Portsmouth, NH: Heinemann, 1987.

Harste, J., K. Short and C. Burke. *Creating classrooms for authors*. Portsmouth, NH: Heinemann, 1988.

Hunt, R. "Could you put in lots of holes?" Modes of response to writing. *Language Arts*, 64, Feb. 1987, 229-232.

Perl, S. and N. Wilson. *Through teachers' eyes*. Portsmouth, NH: Heinemann, 1986.

Smith, F. *Joining the literacy club*. Portsmouth, NH: Heinemann, 1988.